Three Years from Upstate

Three Years from Upstate

Jonathan Regier

Six Gallery Press

2008

for Violaine

Six Gallery Press
PO Box 90145
Pittsburgh PA 15224
www.sixgallerypress.com

ISBN 10: 0-9810091-0-7
ISBN 13: 978-0-9810091-0-0

Printed in the United States of America

Design by Michael & Yonat Hafftka
Cover art: Untitled Watercolor by Hafftka © 2006
Frontispiece: Portrait of Jonathan Regier by Hafftka ©2007

Contents

Three Years from Upstate

Introduction

One of the most exciting moments for a publisher is when he finds a yet un-published writer with a truly original voice. When I first read Jonathan Regier's poetry I was astonished at the creative ease with which his words flow from image to image, from idea to idea. Often breathtaking, his poetry always remains rooted in our most common vernacular—without pretense, yet in no way pedestrian. Out of ordinary subjects he creates magical stories that unfold in the most familiar spaces: the street, our beds, a motel in the countryside.

His rhythms often surprise us with their unusual hops—the very hops that propel narrative poetry, perhaps the oldest of genres, towards an undreamt-of future. When I read these poems—primitive though never inchoate, vague but never incoherent—I always imagine I am hearing them sung. For Regier is a modern troubadour singing to us all, yet his words are hushed, intimate.

Comparing a poet's first book to the work of other great and original writers can be constraining—and a gamble, but a delightful and instructive one. *Three Years from Upstate* is as celebratory as Walt Whitman's "Crossing Brooklyn Ferry" and as mysterious as John Ashbery's "In My Way / On My Way". Regier's uncanny logic also recalls James Schuyler's "Empathy and New Year":

> "...Not knowing
> a name for something proves nothing.
> Right now it isn't raining, snowing, sleeting, slushing,
> yet it is
> doing something."

Regier confesses to being, in his exquisite phrase, "wound tight with uncertainty, as with twine". It is this uncertainty—at once tremulously humble and strangely confident—that irradiates all of his poems and renders each quietly unique.

Michael Hafftka, Brooklyn 2008

New York

Prelude

Three years from upstate is how I feel,
Now living in a city so destitute
Of wanting, that poverty is music to those
In the middle, and the wealthy feel no love,
And the poor have so many choices
Of no choice, and all is therefore right
For all and sundry.

Chapter I

          It was a Sunday,
When we pay for what we did or didn't
With tranquility, with unease toward eve,
And my assumptions were groundless
About the city, and I was wound tight
With uncertainty, as with twine. And I was the man
At the mouth to the subway, on the sill
Of the storefront beside the storefront
Of the HSBC, and what I did there
With a strong cart of four wheels beside me,
A cart filled with newspaper, was a mystery,
Or I was the angel of unmoving, not knowing
A particular angle on the story.

          "Oh, I know without seeing,
I do," said Barnaby, with whom I sat in a low
Manhattan McDonalds, drinking coffee, mine
With three sugars and milk, far down in Manhattan,
On Broadway, in the cleared out district of the night.

"There comes one now," he said, "just the same
As you and me, but with sssssschizophrenia.
No, but really . . . life is like an archery shot,
And heaven help the too strong, too wary:
The space between the bow and bowstring is,
I've always thought, a gateway."

I was tempted to tell Barnaby he didn't know squat,
And that if he lived in a big house, if he went
Down the stairs as another went up,
The cloistered ear, according to position,
Would guess at one, and only one, direction.

*

Unctuousness of the subways, beyond midnight,
In the earliest morning, when the steel and plaster
Do their rotting, when I felt better in a sleeveless shirt,
In a station like an iron shoe, buried askance in the earth,
In the backyard, by the family dog;
Unctuousness of the tunnels, of the air tubes that pump
Stale air beneath the East River, a vein of memory,
A library of unremembered vision, precious,
Bearing odors of holiness, a catalogue of a catalogue
Of the cards that suffer the encoding of days,
The tiles brown as banana skin, all glued together
In the humidity of the walls, passed over
By traipsing fingers, by pensive fingers,
By fingers old and young; the whole uptown scheme
Is sanctified by what is lost, where the few of us
On the platform, lay as old lettuce in a sandwich,
Smeared over in dressings.

                                        A heart is worn on the foot,
Pumping an underground oil through sensations
Of iniquitous clarity, of the day, of the night. Don't
Seize up with the bells of a fire truck. There's an ambulance
At the corner of my block. God help me.
God grant me health, which is golden, truly.
Let me not be a miser with it. Eudemonia.
I'm too young for that. Let me be frictionless
As in a dream. Black oil. Gold from the ground.

At the corner is a stop light. I had a conversation.
Kinesophobia, that's the topic of my dissertation,
And the very worst cases, she said, we cannot move them
From bed. I made a visor of my palm to see you,

For I don't know you, though romance becomes you.
A Mexican, he's turning the street below him
By the wheels of his bike. Please step on the sidewalk.
He may catch on his apron. He'll take you with him.
In this city, she said, there's no cushion. It's all a matter
Of money. But the F for failure comes like honey.

Chapter II

Barnaby hath sat five years to the day, is wicked
In himself and all his works, is a friend
Of the penniless, a jerk to the seine of bulbs
Bought with riches, laid over marshland, star-land, pasture.

"Gardeners," he said, "of assonance. Frequenters
Of the palace of downtrodden chocolate fixes,
Let me buy a lottery ticket tonight. I shall win
The tar in my lungs. My head shall fall
To the kitchen table. Yet I am not a king.
Oh my neck shall follow - " (thunk)

"What?"

"Oh my neck should follow -"

"That's natural."

"Oh my neck should follow -"

"I'm happy to help you,
Barnaby, dear child of poverty and innovation,
The sole progeny of what stumbles and is unwanted,
The patrimony of a night on the town, of coins enough
Barely to get drunk, the static residue of a monorail
Through an old steel city, whose historic waterfront, all agree,
Is in need of restoration."

"Oh my neck should follow -"

"Yes, for the centipede is the creature most in line
With his own wishes, most true of body and mind, an arrow
Shot from the hoary hands of Nature, most true to himself,
A vision of the strong line of sight, an embodiment of that vision,
An army of legs, yet a single mission, a sweathouse of stitches,
Yet utterly whole in the first dimension, unwholesome brute
Of utmost precision."

"Oh my neck should follow -"

"You, Barnaby, are a constellation of a single point,
You are an Ursula in a bucket of soup, and the ladle is lost.
You are an astronomy of some poor pre-Socratic,
Smote in the head by an anvil."

"Oh my neck should follow -"

"But I have read your cravings and deliver, shall provide
Pennies for your probability, white lights for your lungs,
For we are friends, for we have no lovers, but are vagrants two,
Emissaries of a forgotten court, craftsmen of sound
And sense - and where the pen leads us on - Don't say it!
Let us only be gone from this bodega, for you are stoned.
Let us pay the good Turk what he wishes and go."

Chapter III

Ring once or twice.

Stop the ringing -

Ring once more. I am not young. Her father is not home.

I am not sad. I am not alone. A good friend is with me.

> What is the meaning of fasting?
> I would fast for three nights
> Out of pure happiness for love.
> Tonight is the night of her party.
> She will answer the door.
> She will have spent the afternoon
> Preparing.

A man prepares for this
By being strong. He thickens up:

> He, bedecked in ropes of ivy,
> Beseeches the doorbell, humbly,
> To convey his thrill
> To the lady.

> She must answer with airs
> Of an estate, or cathedral.
> She must be an architect
> Of the gentleman's mind.
> She must be the foreman
> Of tremors in open space.

> The strong man, roped over in green,
> Will sit on the couch. He will chat,
> Take food from a bowl, cross his legs,
> Stand up to greet. The leaves will stand up
> To sniff. They will luxuriate, or look dumb
> As an office fern.

"I find it so easy to talk with you."

April.

The tree has a mind of man, you know, but we've yet to find it in the pulp.
"I likewise find it very easy to talk with you."

The tree has a mind of man, you know, and yet no purpose in the mind of man.

I saw the oak of the estate. I saw it even in that dead cathedral at Reims.

Chapter IV

My specimen of antiqueness, the horns trumpet our affinity
At Hicks, over the ravine of the freeway. The storefront church
Of Spain. A street fair. Supposition. While I have a hook-up there,
For you it's easy. But for me, I need a fair pipe of liquor—
Supposition—in the palace of karaoke.

                                    "What bites at the heel
Is what scares us from Sorrow. This is not true."

                                  "Now,"
Said Barnaby, "it was no help for Melville's son, the mockery
From his father, well said or not. Cynicism is all very typical.
Data collection. What ordinary thing can perform magic
Of terrific value? There is boredom on the veneer of the sea,
A black dust, and to whisk it off takes pipes of celestial sound,
I mean the silver spouts."

                       "Barnaby, I'm having trouble thinking. The bartender
Is staring. Let's find a seat further back, or let's talk softly."

"Stop," he said. "Here's something from my own man. Please take it.
Your lady left our bright region. Only gods live long enough here."

"And it was some doubt, some fleck of craving
For another. Some series of weeks where I said naught but dullness,
That she thought me mistaken. Some kiss unintended for her,
Who was effectively my wife. We woke up in my place near the port.
The white liner, a wash of white hull, stacking terraces
Swept backward from the bow, were offered over to my windows
Once a week. You'd think that enough. Or was it the contradiction,
To see me curdling a new day in my gullet, against such a scene?
I honor what I want. I don't need consummation."

                   "Are you thinking plain yet?"

"No."

         "More bitterness?"

"Yes, and I could fuck any woman I saw."

"Here comes one now," he said. "Marjorie, this fellow here
Is downright fighting against himself."

"Oh, Marjorie, you're nothing but
A lovely sock!"

"Marjorie," he said,
"Pronounces names with a stutter. Her loyalty is boundless. She will walk
Wherever with a man, so long as his pace stands in reason."

"Marjorie, then,
Is quite like me. Guileless in the face of evil. Anti-eloquent.
A soul chiseled with function. A swift kick. Or turning on a dime."

"Behavior," he said, "liable to bring trouble."

"Oh, Marjorie,
I demand your council. Oracle of oracles, better than any goddess,
Your strength is with the great and small alike, with the conquering
As with the downtrodden. You are at once with the man who flees
And the man who pursues. You are hung upon the place of fire
Yet filled with sweetness. Please tell me what to do."

"Marjorie,"
He said, "has spoken. What is the mere body of sight? What
Is cast off? What wrecks the carpet with smell, or else is buried
In the backyard, below the oak? What but recollection? What
But memory? It is a sheath, a banana skin. It is thrown
In the corner, turns overripe. It is a maggot. It stitches
The sun-side of an old steak. And who can approach his argument
Like Decomposition, so steadily, proffering a sureness found
Not in stuttering spring, nor in youth, whose uncertainty
Is a cold moss of March, the green who crumbles the rock? Thus
If you want her, it must be gloom where you go, the land
Of the sodden chaste."

"But can you pinpoint the location

Of this rabbit hole?"

"I should lead you by steps, if you were running -
But the sheet of earth swings out beneath you. See how you're floating.
The old waters will take you. A man so heavy will go where he needs to."

Chapter V

Already, the lights of the city were smeared on my face
Like war paint, and I was diving to the gates where
Five palms were lifted upward, from the low mid-level of the sea,
And each palm swayed lightly; each swayed in accord
With the others, making small adjustments
Of geometry, for the design must keep its import
And not snap against the swells. Geometry
Of sales folk in a shop, will keep the crowds from advancing
Or buying the belts. Geometry of two in a bar
Will keep the foreign Lothario at bay. The language
Of what is called soul, of some essential in-body, barely
Of quality, yet a thickness of shadow, a bit of contentment, a bit
Of enmity, strung together in succession, like a film, but dropped on the floor,
A narrative lost, a bundle of color and image, yet without sound,
The language of this peculiar thing, though a mess in itself,
Is a matter of precise geometry, should it live in a skull, when it talks to another,
A communication through distance and position, upon a board
Of finite space. This is the first language. It is known by insects
And fish. We are born with it, and refine it within its natural scope.
I tell you, these palms, while I descended, these hands held up to me,
They would let me pass, yet no creature could rise through them,
Such was their net of suggestion.

      Then I remember the sound of a dog.
A scratching. Both of us in a black box of slight dimension.
And he felt me, set off a terror of whines and whinnies.
I wasn't scared. I said, "Hush now," and he was
Adequately quiet. And that was passing.

      Then it was a long time
In those tunnels. And I tell you I saw the ghost of her.
We did a great deal of talking, but always in delusion,
And what was said was immediately forgotten. Everything forgotten
We said again. I believe we lost the good of our minds.
We forgot that we hid together, and still spoke, the one
To the other. And there were steel girders in that place,
And we were heavy with the water that came down the walls
And turned them to rust. I don't know how long this was.
Three hundred years.

Chapter VI

And then I was brought to the chamber
Of the king and queen, told to bow. A voice made a sound:
"Imposter." That was me. My whole life was theirs to take.

"Yes. I'm the one who keeps his suit of skin. And nerves made my stay
Unpleasant, yet gave me a certain will, a focus, an ambition
Far out of season. I've come to take her, the one with whom I was found,
And to return her. I shall not swim up through that ocean either.
I've found your trap door. In my reveries here below,
I've seen how easy it is to come out the other side."

The king made a glance
At his queen.

"Yes," I said, "and I've never seen such a pair
Of sewer rats, you and your Proserpine. Father Time and Lady Death,
The ones to whom we have nothing to say. You, sir, put the ore in the bore
Of the iron age. Do drop your scepter. Your lady does not love you,
But only the firmness of what is stupid and certain and soon coming,
For she is herself a too steady lay, and shall have it quickly
Or never. I, for one, fell asleep inside her."

"Really," said the king,
"Look, dear, this man will talk like a man who spites us for choosing
To withhold our power. He does his dignity a certain honor.
He bids it ado when it leaves."

"Imagine that I'm out in the parking lot
Of a grocery store. I'm pushing my cart to the car. Now, do I deliver
A stanza of honor, if at that moment, some great beast, a pterodactyl,
Plucks me up and flies me away, takes me to his nest, picks me apart
By the stone beak of his absurdity? To be unstrung in pain
By a brute anachronism, by a farce of terror, by a warty face
From a children's tale, that is the sense of us who live in your reign.
And don't say how you incite desperation, how you therefore
Fill my head with wisdom and sharpen my eye. You and your wife
Are as witless as a bone mace, as a stoning parade of townsfolk
Screaming a law old as superstition."

"I'll tell you, traveler," said the king,
"There's a suavity in what we do."

"There's a suavity," I agreed,
"In keeping your mouth shut and letting other people scream."

The queen turned to me. "Young man," she said, "I admire your idiocy.
Now, listen well. I will tell our good use plainly. All works of mind possess
A teleology, a drive, a contradiction, a form of life in the future state,
Which is unquenchably close. Now, as the tribe of wolf is unable
To feed itself at once, and the winter was hard, it should be that a percentage
Falls ill, that a great many are hunted by hardship, and that all arrive here in the end.
But man has a greater hunger than the merely bestial. Therefore, enlightened
Population control, the combing of fitness in society, while meeting excellent standards
Of greed and necessity, both spiritual and physical, this is, in fact,
The alpha and omega of economy. And I'm not sorry."

*

But they gave my lady back to me, perhaps as a gift
For the conversation. And they were clear of the one condition,
That I should take her hand and not doubt her,
But lead her out the way I'd seen, with my living vision.
And I knew the way out: I was sure I remembered.
If she or I should trip, we won't falter. We will push on,
Continue. We two are together, and I have a few days left
In the bosom of nature.

Youth

Quietus is of all the atoms
The fastest and the rarest, coming thin as a wire
In a music hall, and bowling over the princess,
And bowling over the player,
Still a boy, who is now a sagging moustache
      With only an I.
This is the word that got me up. This is the one
That I am up against, the one I lay against
When I'm dry. I have not had enough of it.
If it weren't such a pacifist,
I would let it punch me in the nose another time.
      If it didn't coax me to sleep,
I would call it Senescence and Shriek.

In Another Man's House

Really, I'll ask you serious questions. Do you cheat on your girlfriend?
Are you married? Can you make ends meet, ethically?
They say we consume most of what we have, financially, no matter what we earn a year,
But I'm not convinced. I'm not the only rich man here who makes so much more
Than he can spend. Just the other day, I bought a chandelier in another man's house,
And I'll keep it there. I'll pay rent on the ceiling space, though the matter, I think,
Might rise swiftly through the courts, once I get my papers together. And why not buy
The flower that lights the dancing place? I'll knock every stupid moth away
That's clung to the two lips of his wife when she greets me.

The Country

Scene I

Five and half acres keep me outside, in the north
Of the state. A low rent keeps me there.
I've lost my feeling of being alive.
The throated forest can warble at night
Like a roadside branch.

The only living thing is a dog out back.
He survived two winters on his own, people say.
He dug himself in, beneath the warm cement
Of a neighbor's house, far away. The sky
Turns dark blue on the snow. He lost his marbles a bit.
He's half-wild now, but he won't bite.

Self-pity and a hard day. I lay on the couch.
Five minutes' time, turn off the light.

        If eyes are shut
        Yet see clear
        Shadows on the basin,
        On the hemisphere
        Of sleep, leaves
        Over waters held in the lids,
        The presence of love
        Is near.

Easy pleasure.
        Of all the small choices I couldn't parlay
        Into greatness, they were never.

(It's a cheap kind of wisdom,
Knowing violent men. You can learn it soon
If you don't know it yet. It's helpful in this world,
Though it won't make you strong.
Sometimes you float on top of it.)

"Oh David, small and sad."

"A girl like you is real because she needs to be.
We're very soft, the two of us, and I'm as timid as fourteen.
The skin gives way to skin, and the heart
                                              is more of the same within.
                        Let me have comfort,
A temptation of peace after peace after peace, blown
          To a redness on your little expanse."

"David, my dear lost lover?"

"Is that the hound who whispers?"

"No, you fucking jerk, it's Christine Desalva!"

"Bah! She's dead!   *   I sit up instead!"
                        "Dear David,
I've spoken to myself in loneliness too.
The magician is well past us, his fingers
On his knees, thinking of his laundry or
What sort of query a rabbit is . . .
When you get right down to it. Quickness?
Another meaning of whiteness? Something beyond
What you can just now touch? A pretty haunch
In fleetness suspended, just at the very cusp
Of the trimming that keeps the hollow from diving
Beyond forever? To take it requires foresight
Ahead of time. What can you do?"

                "You can throw a rock at it."

"You hit her, you hit me! David,
                        For the love of God,
                        Please turn on the light to see!"

"Christine, ghost of my old lover?"

"My wedding day is on the fourth of the month, second month on the year!"

"Should we go in the dark?"

"It's a distance from your house, you know, in a mid-winter's bower.
The stage is being set there. I'm gonna tie my life to nobility! I'd like some coffee.
I'd like to leave in an hour."

Scene II

"The stars are wild tonight, and the air is in frost.
I'm stepping on old pine cones through the snow.
I like the texture of these evergreens in my flashlight.
I mean that there's no problem anymore.
My coat is barely enough, and we're far from home."

"There's not anyone you know."

"To the stamp of a buck's hoof in the path,
Filled over with mire, little wings doth flit
And start, and meet in kindness a lady in shawls,
And wet awake her lips. Snow from sky.
'Tis the time. Ice floes stand in the harbor.
A foreign people arrive, their legs insensate
With travel. They wait for personnel
To let gates down. Life is not so long.
They are here, colonize a quarter, live
With quaint habits, amongst themselves.
In time they integrate, make law. It doesn't matter.
Where the buck goes, so goes the man.
Her husband is the green hunter."

"You mean you're thinking about marriage in general?
Or civilization? Put on your gloves.
The earth is very cold. Aren't you curious?
Is that enough, to know the earth is very cold?
You brought an end to yourself, on your own terms.
You brought an end to yourself, precipitating my own."

"People do what they do. The bear noses its kill.
The monkey can caress with sign, can lie and steal,
And protect its boy to the death. We stand on top
The collective greatness of the beast, who plies
A grand apparatus of choice, within his sphere,
And I within my own."

"You're so full of shit. You loved me, sure. It's just that
You were always in love. You love glory,

Or you love a girl. You can't be alone. You make up grace
To crawl between a lady who's not more or less
Than any other gracious guest."

"May I have a cigarette?"

"Will your hands be cold?"

"They're fine. And Oh you make a beautiful ghost."

Scene III

"The trees open here onto a little plain, covered in snow,
Where we'll meet an emissary of my boyfriend's court.
I wasn't given a map. I was told that you could bring me
To the first of the places I need to go."

"And what?"

"We're supposed to stand in the middle and wait."

"I'm sure it's pretty, with the tall pines like this
In a sort of ellipse around us. Although a little disconcerting.
The shape could be a little less wobbly, I think, as whenever I raise
My eyes to the heavens, I feel like I get stamped in the head
With drunkenness."

"Don't worry. He's supposed to meet us soon, I guess."

"Hello!" cries the little man with ferret's face.

"Hello!" we cry back.

Then the plain is quiet as ice. The sky is black:
"I wish for silver Artemis to soar up
And call forth her highwaymen of song."

"Such a one were you?" he asks. "Roving man of the moon?
Cheerful stranger, dangerously up to task regarding
The tidal metaphor, and wheeling happenstance like a shank?
Are you the militia man, enforcing watery give and take
Of knowledge and possession?"

"No. This is how I am: when armored Artemis
Unsnapped herself like a cameo, I fluttered away.
I'm as tenderly upset as a girl. What about you?"

"A man of good relations am I. An office
Of oak in my home. An international map on the wall
Over my desk. The skin of a bear? No."

"And," said Christine, "he's reputed to read minds.
I've seen it myself. Guard well that black seed
Behind your left eye. Was it from a pomegranate?"

"But don't you ever sympathize," I ask,
"Toward a crisis of identification?"

"Never at all. No, not in the least. If anything
It piques my distinctiveness: you maybe don't know
What I know of loneliness. Every action of the diplomat
Is made from it."

"Sir, that's intense. If a touch condescending."

"No, not in the least. How can you speak for good cause,
For truth and peace, yet never speak as yourself, yet understand all things
Of the men at the table, and so speak naturally, as you almost might,
If it weren't for a touch of artistry—that you can never be rid of?"

"I'm not sure. Christine, would you agree?"

"David, it's impossible to argue. The empire is beautiful, and requires different services
From different people."

"Yes. I guess it does.
I'm so out of it. I'm so American I should be living in my own fucking country.
What they claim about us being young when we got here, being a young land -
No. We were pregnant with frenzies, sick in health, hale in sickness.
We broke this down, built it up, caught all the old diseases.
But what was our one single reason?
It doesn't exist. If I'd been alive then, I would have said,
'I just got mixed up in it. Fuck you. It takes all kinds.' "

Scene IV

"The hound is with us on a little path
Dark with overhanging branches. Spars
Thick around us, obscure the vistas.
Christine is ahead of us. The hound
In a rough way keeps her company."

"That's weird. A second ago, I saw nothing."

"It's ok. If your seconds are so meaningful,
You're living well. I'm joking. You see the tail
Of smoke there, the ghost of a scar, a hundred yards
From here? It shows the location of a small hut. Christine
Can wait until we're back, and she'll be fine. You'll meet
The guard of our peculiar border, and then we'll continue.
Watch your step. The gentleman on duty tonight,
You may want to know that he's got a record
As fine as a silver trophy, but sustained some grievance,
Not for the work, but for what the work connoted."

"Customs? Is he a sensitive guy?"

"Not that. You'll find out that our borders are defined—
But I wouldn't lead you to believe they're deduced
Geographically. They're deduced, a reality that necessitates
Provisions regarding fact collection. Our men
Must live in your place and mine, at once, and be equally adept,
And their alliance must be unquestionably ours,
In so far as they keep themselves morally fit.
The other dissent, the ideological, we don't experience that."

"And what about him?"

"He was shocked. Instead of living two lives at once, expertly,
He lives two times at once. He's here, and he's in memory,
But memory he traduces with the present. He's a seer of sorts.
He's at least dependable enough. He faithfully reports anything curious
From this blank region. Please don't be surprised - "

At once the door of the shack—it jumps
And swings to. Snow falls from the roof.
A tall man with a trim gray beard, forty-five years
To his name, peaks out.

"What the hell?" he whispers. "Please, my hearing
Is very keen."

"We know," says the advisor. "I wanted you to meet the dear friend
Of Christine. He shall be visiting our country."

He glared at me. "Scumbag," he whispered, "for doubting yourself,
For waking up from a dream, like the rest, not knowing
Who you are, in fear of yourself. Use this." And he smacked his head.
"Compile a dossier based on your past. Other people in loneliness,
They will forget you. They will misremember you in their happiness,
You whore, because you can't enforce reason—reason, that spreadsheet
Of goodly proportion, telling you what a person really is,
Or the percentage of their completing a certain task, of their rising
Above themselves, at last, of accepting like a drowning man
The accumulation of need, flaw, dream, that led to this choice
At this time, exactly as it has from day to day, cigarette to cigarette, or
Turning the car-keys, just now, or yesterday, and picking up the kids."

At once, the gentleman's head was retracted. The door to the shack
He quietly shut.

"Now," said the advisor, "I want to show you the shock I mentioned.
It's good to note eloquence, and to trace it to its heart and hearth."

The advisor walked to the door and opened it. He gestured.
I shook my head. He gestured again and we went in.

There was a plain farmhouse desk, very neatly kept. A black stove
Was a stout friend, standing against the back wall, between an army issue cot
And where the border guard sat, on a stool, with nothing in his hands.

"Now," said the advisor, "tell us what your dream is."

When the guard spoke, it wasn't the same voice as a minute before,
But a measured voice, a good colonel's voice, in a radio play squawking
Upon an old radio set.

"The reasonable assumption," he began, "is that our guy,
Who was supposed to find us at the office
Of the lieutenant governor of this place -
If that's the right translation - is it?
Same cretin in any case -
Our guy was supposed to meet us here and collect his stuff -
He's probably in a four foot cell,
Electrodes hanging off his nuts
And two of his nails in a cactus pot.
But he was a good spy, wasn't he?
A good man of variable dimension is hard to find,
And I'm reminded of a certain saying. Here's Edmund Burke:
'When bad men combine, the good must associate . . . '
I forget the rest. Et ainsi de suite. The point being
That bad men combine. Did you know they line up and lay on
Wound to wound? They're like the claymation germs
From Sesame Street. One second they're an indissoluble heap,
Then they repatriate themselves, and go on about the special rights
Of each and each and each . . .
It's hard work to be a spy, but you get to sleep.
The days are confusing, but you get to keep the rings."

"Thank you," said the advisor, "for sharing with us
A drama that defines you."

He gestured to me and we left.

Scene V

"You're very safe," said the advisor to Christine, "though cold.
The curtain is always drawn around the kingdom. The unwilling,
The stupid, never draw it back, though the treacherous might, by chance.
They say that wolves pace our perimeter. These are, in point of fact,
Only men—inspired, sure, but not productive yet.
Men, as the expression goes, grasping at straws. Well,
It's better to say that they're in a stage of life when - "
He smiled, " - when the definition of beauty is:
A form making you desperate. They're easy to control.
A simple sign, a learned wink -" The advisor raised his hand,
"And we'll take whatever help we can get.
They tear the pretenders apart, and their claws have a way
Of catching on the impure of heart."

"I hadn't heard about those," said Christine.
The hound lay down in the snow, his nose between her boots.

"No, no," said the advisor. "We'd better be on the move.
We're on our way to meet the king."

"Yes," said Christine, and she put her hand on the dog's head.

"I don't know," I replied. "But I kept on with them."

Whatever vague trail we followed through the woods
Took us to a point where a sharp way intercepted us,
Perpendicular to our walking, which had turned as much to ambling
As the snow flakes lilting here and there
From a sky that looked clear. I felt like we could have gone on
Endlessly, in a lullaby down, had this new route not
Cut into us. The advisor halted us. Unsteadily, I swung round
Almost ninety degrees. We hove to anew.
I felt gravel beneath my boots.

I'm not sure how long we went on the path. Half a mile, I suspect,
Taking into account the silence, also my stinging fingertips.
I shouted hot breath on them, through the lining of my gloves,
Then shuttled them into the pockets of my pants.

And we were looking out at vast lawns, a property
Well-kept, of incredible dimension. Rolling Elysium,
Decked over with glittering whiteness. Flickering flames
In those glass bird-boxes of iron streetlamps, led us to a dell,
A small wood within the fields, and a pretty Victorian house,
Three stories, in the obscure center of it.

"Now," declared the advisor, "we knock."

"If he'll let us in," Christine laughed, "why not?
Yikes. I guess I expected it to be swank like this."

"You're so honest," smiled the advisor, "it's refreshing."
He lowered his voice. "I'll tell you . . .
You've done wonders for him."

Scene VI

The King was in his bedroom upstairs, about to go to bed.
The butler showed us up and led us through.
We barely had time to admire the ivory men stacked
On small bookcases, throughout the home, a populace
Under reading lamps, on mantles above a fireplace,
Or thronged alongside candlesticks in the saloon,
On liquor shelves with silver tracings, the patterns made
By a fern, by figure skaters on a silver pond. The little men stood
Having disagreements, or deep agreements (communicated, naturally,
With discretion), among forks and spoons
On the drying racks in the kitchen, or among goblets
And porcelain plates, on that stupendous dining room table,
A Greenland of burnished oak. They were paupers and bankers,
Chefs and waiters, bus drivers and livery men, Indians from old Montana,
Or coachmen for Louis Quinze, or superintendents
Of Brooklyn tenements, circa 1956. Imagine a type.
He had his representative, maybe in a closet,
Top shelf, beside a pile of maps. I can't imagine
How he wasn't there.

We didn't remove our coats. The cold
Still flapped its wings in our skin. We had a cursory look around,
Thanks to the butler. He led us up the stairs,
Back and forth. At the third floor, or maybe the fifth,
We took a corridor moving inward. Soon the butler stopped,
Took in his hand a string suspended
From a ceiling latch. He pulled. The panel opened,
Unfurling a second case of stairs.

"This way," he said. The stairs shook as we climbed them.

The attic was a high chamber, an echo expanse that sat atop the manor.
It was narrow at the edges, but it peaked along the center seam
Of the building, according to the shape of the roof. The wood beams
Were unfinished, the floor boards bare, excepting the few rugs
Laid down for the comfort of the king, and excepting, I suppose,
The dust that settled from the air.

The young king sat at the edge of his bed.
"I woke," he said, "to meet you. Is that your dog," he asked,
"Baying outside, not far in the distance?"

"Yes." Just then, I remembered about the wolves who were men,
And I looked at the advisor. But he was gazing intently at a glass
Filled with water, on the night table's edge.

"Sit down," said the king to Christine. She sat beside him.

I spoke. "Enough! Finally and forever, I demand to know this post,
The name of your country, its imports and exports,
Whatever they be, and the extent of your reach, internationally."

"Oh? This is the house of the kingdom of sleep.
For what it's worth, my power is upon the cities,
Upon the dark countries that go on endlessly between.
I'll tell you something else. It's a stand-in sort of power.
I don't do the officiating, and policy is beyond me.
I'm another sad metaphor. You wake up knowing and not knowing.
You go to work. You look through your neighbor's eyes
And regard yourself. The dove of the day is well sunk
Below the waters, and we'd be happy to take off for good.
Have you noticed something else?
We've as much volition at two or three in the morning
As we do at noon, if not more. I'm glad universities still pay
For questions concerning inside and out.
You're a sheet transparency, hung to dry. The sun sinks.
The moon slides along the planet. Sleep is so spread around these days,
Shot through with caffeine, so always there in a smog,
Where does it live? I'm an actor running for president. Please understand:
The cast of players sit and smoke on benches, in the ceaseless backrooms
Of the theatre, thinking of synthesis, if they're good,
Or aping the TV movies of boyhood—that's if they suck.
Too bad the ape in us is long gone. Well, I'm on my way out.
The girl's coming with me, but I'll tell you what . . . "

"What?"

"I'm about to escape: it'll be too late by the time you know how. Be happy for that,
Be happy for felicity, which sets us all free, at least till deliberation reaches
Maturity. The galaxy goes round, on a heliotropic stem. Yes, it does.
The lotus grows from the swamp. Etcetera.
It's when you're sunk—it's then—
Your forefathers are waiting upon your thoughts.
          So good night and good riddance. My advisor will show you the door."

Gospel

From mirror to mirror of a farmhouse lot
  From stone to stone to gramophone
  erosion
        in silver patricide
from outer space   finally
      upon our candle nights of Christmas
      Sunday barbeques of liberty.

Innovation is roundabout
as a twister in a teacup.
Innovation brings our hands to our heads.
    I have invented a game which can work no matter who comes to power,
artistically or politically, and no matter their device.
  This game is one to heighten your sensations
& to vivify your relaxations.

Start with a black box and sit inside it. This is the "tester." Sing for the tester like me,

Little neurosis,
      Sound of wine glasses played
      Circular, with a wet finger,
      Tie a white string round your finger,
      Tap an eyebrow twice before batting—
          Small girl with ribbons and braces,
      What are the things you do to repress the apocalypse?

Now, consider a dearest friend.
Consider his mind and sit and wait.
It is dark in the tester. It is late.
  The game is a game of descriptions.

(hint: time is running out. prepare a description on paper of three objects:
A flower with silver filigree round the petals. A quatrefoil in silver, gateway of the gods. An-
other friend.)

Then, if your description is nice and clear,
Should your friend be in his hell one day,
Should his eyes be ruined and a Trinity appear,
      Yet he shall know without his sight,
      He shall know without a doubt, as by taste of salt,
      He shall know what is the other so near to him.

Fantasia

Each kingdom enters its enlightenment. As for mine,
We'll mount a great shield as a prospect for peace.
We could develop the technology. From sea to sea
The heart of liberty shall live, ensconced in a thunderhead
Of transparent strain. If it sounds like a scheme baked up
By some guys in a bar, but the land of self-sufficiency
Is not a drunk. We make good choices. We don't owe money
To every homegrown pimp in our yard. We don't answer
To an oligarchy of addiction. We don't stumble toward the pen
And desk of every new prescription. We don't long for transcendence
In this life, but lovely relations.

2007

And of the lofty creature, of flat out Dominion,
I once saw sign of him, Tuesday morning,
And his ways need little expostulation.

I saw sign of him in the winter,
      On a street by the river in Brooklyn, by the ports, a mile
From the big cranes.
                  And the street was
Run across by sunlight, by sun-trucks clattering,
By black people, by the white people there, by two workmen loading oranges off a truck
In the gelid air, talking Haitian French—everything was a noise,
A tin can noise, a clatter of light through a wineglass filled with water,
                  a seagull thrown arch-wise in its tranquility, a discus
         in skies of grape hyacinth

The Hunting of the Beast

I.

It's good to belittle Death if you're young. Whatever creature takes you
Has zero care for words that bring consolation, and won't hold them against you.
Even murder, the coldest murder, is a force attending to its work, which is to birth
A state of absolute tension, and to bring forth this muscled and hungry kid
From the queen of what exists but pretends not to exist, called Deception,
The second daughter of Nature, after Contrition, who lays hapless brilliance
Upon hapless brilliance, always hoping to make amends, bringing outrageous new food
To the banquet, to the luxurious everyday massacre, wishing for cake-layer stasis, or wishing
By a half-notch to reduce the general hunger—and she won't mind if you mention
The pretty aptitude of her sad and serious expression.

II.

New days pass quickly. The women on TV,
They present the weather, wear their clothes and hair
In blameless fashion. New days or old.
Old days pass quickly. Whatever guile is inside me
Resolves itself. To be with the girl or not, to be with
                                        my Contrition,
Seems like picking up the glass of gin and seltzer.

III.

What's going on here? Nothing. Bite marks like a dog.
Newsmen speculate. My motel room is America's last
With a black and white TV, so I spend the afternoon in bed,
And newsmen talk. Experts have no cradle wherein to lay the infants
Of their conjecture. A large cat might have done it. A tiger.
The nearest zoo is so long away, it's got to be a big dog. Possibly,
A bear. He would have drifted so far from the parks, a hundred-fifty miles,
At the least. And I haven't heard science on the marks.

This country is the plains. October. The fields, desiccated.
A pig pen by a brown pond. A light several miles out.
The heavens bear down, unbelievably, on the land.
About the expanse you could ask many questions or none.
I'll ask.

IV.

I saw three signs on the day of the murder. The first,
Parson's ice cream rolled by—I mean a truck, distributing
Ice-cream from the factory to the various shops, and I know
An ice cream maker. He's unconscious with good luck.

The second sign, a telephone florist on the radio, talking of love,
Saying, Don't grow old and bitter with uncelebrated love, saying
Don't let your neighbors perceive an end to your love, for if they perceive it,
Their suggestions may pick through your love . . . as honeybees made from cement,
Collecting heat in their legs, house heat and sweetness; these honeybees,
They'll even make warm carpets cold. They can't grow warmer on their own.

I saw a third sign, a greeting card that told me to get lost, a typically
Bright exhortation, here rendered unlovely, unloving, by the inside picture,
A gray truck. Understand, a day later, I went to the house—it was done over
In past tense. I stood behind the police tape, had a look. The red paint was astute enough
To fade rather than chip. And the one front window showed a narcoleptic eye
To the page that hangs aloft and asks not to be read, asks not for anything, being
A meek end-page of the universe. But in the yard, left of the door,
A frontispiece of white and purple flowers—long stems, numerous petals—
Blew upward from a garden space, a little plot, four posts hammered down,
And a shiny, pink cloth, tied from corner to corner. In the driveway
Stood a grayish truck.

—So, I said to myself, the guy had a wife or lover. Where is she now?

V.

The squirrels frolic in the back lot of my motel. After an hour
Of watching them give chase, leaping from a chain link fence
To a garbage pail, you'd feel like spending an hour at the mall yourself.
This too small city scatters sunlight like tin, makes it thinner, less hot,
Like in the morning, when the sleeper, flat-awake, runs the shower,
Considers rightly the coldness of the tub, feels the cold flecks from the water,
Wonders if the heater's finally shot, if today's the day it happens—
And what's the cost? Small time money from a small time job?
Yes and no. Not a small time life.

(I told you what I found and go to sleep.)

VI.

Cold well water in the dark, well-founded and well-sprung.
The water drawn from the well is always cold.

Burden comes from cold water, all features
Of praise, fascination, happiness. I sometimes believe so,
Not really believing. Cold water is nothing but cold.
We're in such cahoots with the body, the mouth says to fill
The mouth with cold water. The throat says to swallow it fully.
Don't you approve of this? I give my complete approval, personally,

And wonder why the network tragedies roll over the screen
Like a fountain. This isn't cold water. It's all reheated shadow.

VII.

"Did you sleep well, sir?"

Any letters would do.

"Let's check. No, not in your slot. Nothing yet."

Please, in that case I barely slept.

"The less a lullaby works, the tougher we get."

That's a line of bullshit, friend. What's going on here?
That damn murder . . . the thought of it keeps me up.

"Keeps us all up. You know how when you're trying to leave
But your granny keeps saying goodbye, over and over,
And will you ever just get out the door? It's like that,
The tragedy saying goodbye, goodbye, goodbye, pinching our cheeks again,
Giving our shoulders a hug."

Any news on it?

"Yeah. They've got a guy they think did it."

No kidding.

"That's what they're saying. They just have to catch him first . . .
But at least it means they've got a suspect. I trained to be a cop myself.
I had to leave because of a broken heart."

Really?

"But the guy . . . sounds like a movie . . . he was a drifter, you know.
He was last seen in Fort McMurray."

VIII.

The sky gets so clear and blue on the plains, it's like blue water
In a deep bucket of pitch-black bottom. The domineering universe
Will exhaust you in the plains. There, we sweat more in the skin
Around the heap of coals beneath the heart. There we birth
Those engineers who make a bold career choice, who say yes to the Dept.
Of Defense, who design the next generation of bullet proof vests,
Or the next generation of desert tanks. We rap the knuckles of a morality—
It shall answer. It shall pass the test, offering a safe state,
A solid, square state on the plains. Three choices. Either charcoal-colored loss,
Or cohabitation, or charcoal defeat.

IX.

I'm a professional witness and correspondent. As such, I make the rounds,
And on the new day visit the victim's pastor at the victim's church, asking
Who becomes a target here? The parking lot is empty except for my car
And one other. The place is single story, maybe ten years old, and somewhat
Like a big modular house. It peaks high at the center. The materials are pretty shabby.
But the general shape, a triangle, definitely scalene, is somehow moving.

I go through the door. A coffee machine on a fold-out table. Chairs are stacked
Against a wall. This is the outer hallway. There's a second door facing me.

This is the chapel. A pulpit on stage. A cloth banner above me, reading
"Outside is the War Zone. Must use Peace to survive." I see a man reclining
Against a side door. He approaches.

"Yes," he says, "you're the guy who called?"

He puts his hand out.

Good to meet you.

"I'm sorry. I was praying when you came in. Well, as best as I could.
I'm also pretty tired after what's happened."

I certainly know that.
Do you mind if I ask some questions about Mr. Austin?

"You told me that you were a journalist. I did a search for your name,
Found nothing. No . . . I saw reference to your work. Or something.
It was hard to make out. I'll hope your motives are pure."

I'm sure the police have asked you about Mr. Austen's habits, his
Proclivities and whatnot. Is it possible he had enemies?
I'm just trying to establish, on my own, the likelihood of motives
Easily understood.

"Death. None of us is made for Death. Tell me how you feel about it:
Does it fit you like a glove?"

No. But maybe I'm too unreasonable a case.

The Pastor shook his head:

"Reason? We all point reason toward an afterlife. Reason
Can't be used against itself. Far into the future,
Reason propagates Itself, supposing only life,
Supposing nothing else. Nothing. And what if that first
Supposition were wrong? Is the achievement of man
A whim? No. The stalk of reason goes to the invisible root,
To the materiality of God's work, the historical earth. The bloom of reason
Displays itself, and showing itself delights in Him,
And He, I believe, is delighted, knowing that the bloom,
In showing itself, seeks Him out beyond His work
And finds Him there."

Is that all? Can you think of anything else?

"Nothing except this: the body has its flaws. Imperfectly it's remembered.
Reason has its flaws. Imperfectly it walks and preaches. Compost
Proffers alms to the young. This life is an allegory of the life to come,
This body an allegory of the body, this thought an allegory of thought."

But what about the violence done to Mr. Austen?

"That's actually quite easy—
When we talk about violence, real violence, what we mean
Is the tooth and nail physique of Death. Against sacred and profane,
Against a fork and spoon. To turn these plains into a forehead
That worships its own absurdity, that's the effort of Death."

Pastor, in my opinion you're too abstract.

X.

The Pastor, at last, tipped me off about the girlfriend.
I found her number in the telephone book. I called her up.

"Yes," she said, "you can visit." The police had contacted her.
She'd given a statement. Had she been there that night? Yes.
Was she a suspect? Definitely not. She thought it bizarre
That I was the first news-writer to call.

We scheduled a visit. The following evening. Between eight
And ten o'clock.

XI.

In my dream that night, I was wrongly accused in the populace,
And by the very woman I'd meet tomorrow. Her face
Looked familiar and beautiful, in my dream. Have I finally
Witnessed the face of my Contrition?

Her hair in a single waxy braid
        Hangs against her naked back.
                Hey, Pocahontas, what's with the nautical rope?

Although she perches on my lap,
        Sometimes touching me,
                She almost never kisses me,

My Contrition, why
        Use me, turn against me,
                Touch me sparingly, almost never kiss me?

"That I wanna see more of us in your
        Young senescence, in
                Your blown-out memory, inhabiting

"Our steady success, audaciously transported among
        The ports, among the savage races, taking a peace
                Desired by men all over the world.

"We might denounce our works. Find paradigms to pilot through rock.
        We might lull back and forth on our violence,
                As on the sea. Pique me with stores of wine and houses."

XII.

(The snow coming down on Manhattan,
On a used car lot downtown . . . on those little flags strung over the cars,
And this was in 1976. And the brown bricks of a corner store
Make like the feathers of a wren, also in snow.)

Remember, you're not really lonely. When I was untried,
When my virtue and vice were sleeping under blankets,
There wasn't loneliness yet. Take heart! You're not lonely.
To be honest, you don't even know what sets you apart.

XIII.

"How's the coffee?" she asked. "Hang on,
I'll turn down the TV. I appreciate your interest
In current events. Dave Austen was a good man.
Nobility on the plains. I know to choose the best."

How long have you lived in this house, on the outskirts
Of town, at these outermost lights, overlooking
The flatlands of earth? And why? If you're the one
I think you are, why not a jungle place? Green cushions
Abound. Or with your best machines:
Small sparrows in the tracks and gates and the filthy
Crawlspaces of the city, dangerous with aluminum sprouts?

She gave me a pretty look. "If I had to think of a word to describe you,"
She said, "it would be quaint. No, no. But thank you. My work, I'm sure,
Is great. I think your estimation, however, of my burden
Is incomplete. The problem," she continued, "is that you don't know the half.
There's a genealogy unwritten, unsaid.
                                   I have a sibling. And it lives in the shed."

It lives in the shed?

"That's the secret of this whole mess. No? Is the secret
What you're looking for? It lives out back."

She pulled a tissue from a box. She dabbed her eyes:

"It escaped one night. Followed me . . . to poor Dave's house,
                                                   All the way."

Maybe I'll understand. Dear Contrition, your force
Is disseminated through all living things. I dreamt of you
Last night. But you were smaller. You belonged to me.
It was personal. It was, I suppose, allegory. Your secret
Could be thus among the mortals, no? The secret I'm referring to
Is only Death . . . but what could that mean for you?

Bright Contrition rose. She took my hand, sadly. She took me
To the door. "It's been a pleasure," she said. "It's best if you don't know, body and mind,
How straightforward the bitch wants to get. She'll usually ask you
To simplify. She's the impulse who derides what I made
To stop her. She calls it 'incomprehensible.' She calls it 'perverse.' I
Do what I can with what I have. If I had a can of paint, I'd splatter and mourn,
Recalling birth. I'd draw a girl on a bull. She's wearing lace.
Her knees are up. The heavy haunch of the god, it totters
At the mouth of the deep. The wind that blows the waves to white
Blows up her skirt. Is that perverse? There's a terrible ocean abounding.

"In any case, you'd get ten or twelve critics calling it senseless in parts,
Incomplete, on the whole, showing glimmer of genius, now and then, however
Beholden to Marx. How about 'amateur.' Poor production value. Not systematic
Enough. That's the jibe I hate most. Make enough systematic thoughts,
You've got a row of steak knives coming out. Give the tenor schlock, you start a war.
It's better if the categories come and go, if Twenty-Questions isn't the same
Twice. And what about my creations fucking each other up?
Understand this: until I figure out how to make them stop
I'll work in so many kinks, Death shall never work them out, not purely."

Justice

It's so easy. I've done almost nothing wrong.
I talk thoughtfully. I make decent choices, given
My context. I do errands well, if always later
In the day and week than I'd wanted. With
Uncomfortable dreams but without trouble,
I've become an outlaw to myself.

Why would justice,
My own justice, exact retribution on its source?
It does. As I didn't realize forcefully enough.

I'm sure the law is my own. But I prayed
Lately for strength. So maybe I'm getting strong.
Another young king goes down. He did nothing wrong,
Like me. Except he didn't know himself.
He sought signs and found them, knowing only plots.
This is the way he made decisions:
He set one plot against another, set them to war,
And dropped himself, conclusively, into the deeper plot then,
Being himself the only casualty.

And so I'm an outlaw, instead of dead. I know my mistake.
I confess it, only too late to confess aloud and become
Myself. Don't you see it? I'm the one who holds his life above
Himself. I can rue, equably. I can run.

Why The Fake Flowers

A domestic scene, a sofa scene.
　　　The televangelist calls every evil 'worth killing,'
And those two huddle together, in warming shock of sacrifice,
Each for the other, while her husband whistles
In bathtub water,

'Go ahead and hammer the white to the wall. Fill it
With steel or crossbeams. Just try it. I don't know.
The flywheel is heavy that dredges ghosts from the lake.
The will is old as English oak. There were delicacies, give or take.
I'll overlook how I got here, doing them so well.'

I said to her, 'you're a mid-western girl. here's a dandelion
for you. how pretty etc. & frail.
you're like a japanese poem.'

I said to her, 'why the fake flowers
between me & the world? because I learnt them not being true, nor
having you.'

A Note Aside

Before I go further in this poem, I need to do some sounding out. First, I need to talk about poetry just once. I am a poet, and this particular poem demands that I uncover a method of poetry and my relation to it.

(Poetry is not well-known. It is not well-known, and it is not well-read. So where does that leave me? Well, it doesn't leave me anywhere I wouldn't be anyhow. But I'll give away a secret I know about poems, just because it shouldn't be secret.)

OK, let's first assume that there's a problem. This problem could be of great importance, or it could be of minimal importance. That's irrelevant.

Sometimes I see a problem by my hands; sometimes we brood over mandrakes and mandrake roots in the dark. Some people like these problems the best, but I prefer to wait until the whole scene is emptied out, as it were, which is to say "transparent." But what do I mean exactly? I don't know. But why this method over another? Because I like to "behold," and to behold every side of a problem at once—in the same way that I might behold, for instance, an amber ashtray on a bright day in the park. What's the meaning of "emptied out." Emptied out might be the same thing as "struck through" with light, or it might be that landscapes, all landscapes, turn airily bright in the eyes of an air head.

What do I do for lighting? I use whatever source I have. For men and women wiser than I am, what I call transparent, they call unlit. When I say, "I see," they say, "I don't see." In conclusion, their standards are higher.

Therefore, if I were to write of paradise, that wonderful land would not be suffused with milk, clouds, or colors of lovely pale skin. That's what cataracts make of everything, and a good pilgrim admits to his cataracts (as did the best). As for me, I'd write, "My God, there's clarity here and clarity on earth. Is it woe to me that I can't distinguish?"

Creatures of the Bawd-House

Behold the batman,
Skinny as a scrivener,
The fox-face besmirched
     by shavings,
The wilted membrane
From rib cage to inner arm showing
'Tween slits in his suit.

He reaches for the door,
Comes in meekly,
Sea-sickly—

As if to reel
Were a modest prayer.

"One day
I'll wear a white fedora
With a feather."

The day reaches for the hour,
Backwards.

We worry for a scrivener.

"Assistant!" cries Madame to the bat,
"Copy-master! Strange honeybee of the garden
Of facts! You who know the habit, the heart and bloom
Of data, what makes you so sad?
They say the batman humps like a donkey kicks!
Is that the expression of your proofs?
Why not love the city thusly, instead
Of tutoring our whores biweekly?"

Madame means to say that they're driven into caves,
Those who don't give their love rightly.

            *

In room number three is a rainbow sort of partridge,
Or fancy dove, a fledgling of good looks, if a little thin,

A blond student of rhetoric, cape thrown over wings.

She keeps him waiting, the girl he wants.
She's maybe taking fast money
Down the hall. He looks through the window,
His wings at his chin. The snows are falling.
On Tuesday night he became a thief.

Does he understand? The girl is nowhere to be found.

His muscles hurt from booze and running.
To be miserable.
To fuck up.
What other way to feel one's love
For one's own convicted heart?

Partridge lays on the bed and falls asleep.

                    *

Room five: zebra and zebra
Share a bit of rum, waiting for the lady to come
Service them equally.

"Cheers to the best looking
Cads in town," announce the zebras.

They snort and kick the table,
Their way of agreeing, also of saying,
"And we're not even done!"

But Madame shouts:
"Everyone to the roof!"

Between Zebra and Zebra
A dash is begun.

*

Madame is heard in room number six,
Rather the most teeming room of them all
For reasons we can't mention, owing to the
Bridal connotations of white paper.

(Number six is good for its closet,
A nice place to sit the conniving spouse.)

Mole and Mole. Dr. and Mrs. They like the slick,
The lightless and warm. They like jealousy
Best. And Mrs. Mole, perceiving petting
And breathing from behind the sliding door,
Tears at her vestments. She falls with claws
On her husband, who, at the high-spot of her frenzy,
Explodes. All should sleep extremely well into morning
Instead of waking just before,

Yet Madame cries Fire. The Moles rise greasily,
Rub their eyes, can barely dress themselves.
Dr. Mole complains he needs to use the lieu. They go.

*

The bordello occupies floors twelve and thirteen
Of a tenement house in the muskrat quarter. An old hospital,
That's the look of the house, a composite of four vast
Brick walls, then a great spanning of asphalt on top
Like an airstrip in the fields.

                              Floors eleven and down:
Between each tremendous ceiling is a township of doors
Open and shut, of toys scattered in halls
By washed and unwashed children, of welcome mats
Giving a cold amalgam smell of twenty-five kitchens,
Morning and night, a smell of chicken skins

Fried in vegetable oil. The amalgam sound is not quite
Jubilation. It's a sound of life in the open.

But floors twelve and thirteen,
Deemed unfit for habitation,
You'll find there a different scene.

If no modern spark be communicable,
Then candles suffice for lighting, day and night,
In a bordello. To see a darkness manifest
With the help of five candles drooling wax,
For Madame this was preferable.
The client, therefore, might traverse
Several corridors of trash, find a dusty apartment,
Abandoned many years back, a place of memories
Inaccessible, a simple reference to memory more fruitful,
More complete in its fruitfulness, a tombstone of four who
Still may live, but not quite as they did, and two of them
Are young still, maybe twelve and ten, and common blood, common
Moods, common untellable moods, are in the two of them.

But nothing can be said about a deserted kitchen. Dusty,
By a candlelight or flashlight lit. And the girl leads the client
Through, and they go further. Until there's only one door, and
Behind the door a room, a tacky, a shattering little comfort,
An hour just for him.

*

Says Partridge to Dr. Mole:
"People and places . . . "

                    Dr. Mole inquires:
                    "Do we have rapport?"

          "You were with me when
The sight in my left eye turned so thin and tearful, and the lids
Went thrice their size, and it was like I hung a cherry tomato
In a pouch of skin. I gave little looks through the slit,
And I wept then from the good eye."

"Why, yes! I see you're fit.
But fire plucks at us, means to melt us
To these very stairs! Let's run!"

"Doctor! Why not patience?"

Partridge snatches the flap of his coat.

                    Here's Dr. Mole:
"Do you want to die?
And your whole life ahead?
Make yourself a rill of pleasure . . .
You can fill it, can enlarge it.
You can bury it deep in the earth.
You're a student yet, if I remember,
Find a pass! Fill it and go!"

                 Partridge follows Dr. Mole.

                 *

Partridge falls to the floor, crying out, "How was it the one
Became as two! Bodies of static, you spring from yourselves!"

The zebras continue.
The stampede whacks plaster from the wall.

Partridge flies forward, arresting the neck of the laggard.
The twin gallops on.

"What say you!"

"I demand satisfaction!" cries Partridge.

"On the roof, under clear night, we can have our duel.
Speak quick! But what's the harm I did you?"

"That like bureaucrats and rogues you reproduce!
You take me down, not caring for my hopes!"

With the zebra gone, Partridge talks to himself:

"I can't stay mad. Such a creatures does what it does,
Follows its own logic, as complex a grey-scale
As federal law. And it's better the nations band together so,
By legal expression of common confusion, of policy allied, of
Common spirit and phrase. Better the blaze can't find a good spot
To strike, break through, eat lion-like of muscle and blood."

Partridge shakes his head.

          "I must be scared," he says.

        *

Partridge flies to the crucial ascent,
Spies the final staircase on the dark side
Of a dusty chiffonier. A candle set hastily there
Shows the door open. Madame doesn't merely escape.
She prepares.

       "What's the hurry?" inquires a voice from behind.

Partridge stops, spies Turtle.

Here's Turtle:
"Do you smell fire? Because I don't.
The lady that runs this whorehouse is a nut.
Me, I'm a former family man with a bum ticker,
Which I'm not gonna aggravate for a scam-party
On the roof. I bet she's got the girls lined up
Something beautiful. Thirteen porcelain ponies in the full moon.
When I was your age I said to myself, 'Self,
You'll oppose tyranny of mind till you're deaf and dumb.'
That's why recently I left my wife. And that's why I'm sure
To give the simple life a shot. That's why mud

Is my best friend, and why I spread it around. Mud
Is the first mother. And she's purified. She's canonized.
She's got every kind of life inside her.
Let's get the mud going and see what's what.
We're all reptiles of the swamp. Remember:
It's mud that puts a fire out."

Turtle looks around. Partridge is long gone.

        *

Partridge climbs the stairs now. Steel stairs.
A rectangular well made of steel, painted grey
Decades ago. The paint hangs in leafs. Behold
The fire escape. The sounds of scraping
He cannot place.

                Turtle drags his
Corrugated shell upwards on corrugated steel.
Partridge descends to haul him skyward,
Little by little, turtle spurring much of the ascent:

"Hey-ho, we'll get there! No hurry now!"

           Partridge wheezes for breath.

Until at the topmost stair, Madame puts her big head in the hatch,
Fishes Turtle to the roof,

 Pushes Partridge back:

"Oh, no. Not until you find the girl you were with!"

"But she never came!"

"You say she disappears with her pleasure?"

"No! I never saw her! I'd have carried her!"

"Really," says Madame. Her eyebrows smack together
Like logs in a medieval gauntlet. "But I actually believe you. Have you heard
The meaning of her name? Assure me, Partridge, of no foul play."

"I fell asleep."

"So what if you did? It's obvious you love her."

"But I never met her!"

"Partridge—bird of no subtlety, bird we call stupid—
You never met the one for whom you search?
It's obvious you're lost. Don't you mean to thieve nightly,
To whoremonger nightly? Do you mean to compose nightly
And so compose yourself? When a lady's lost, and moreover
The one you love, it's quite right to assume that her liege,
Meaning you, is also lost. And therefore you stand like a shadow of lost
If you've really never met her."

Partridge looks past Madame. The stars seem to support her
As joints of a chair. Otherwise, maybe she'd fall upward.

"Well," says Partridge, "I'm at least an expert on surrender."

"Nicely put. Scrivener!" she cries, and the bat appears
Behind her. "You shall go with Partridge!
Look here! You'll at last have real writing and adventure!"

Winter

I.

Little boots are sure reassuring when little mitts and shovels bury us with snow.
Well, I'm holding my chin in my hands, and for all the world I'm lying on my stomach
Like a dog, all jangled nerves and nothing to do. Tomorrow is called the winter solstice.
Tonight is called the night when the solstice hasn't even come.

Please let little children bury me with snow when I practice this.

II.

Do you remember saying what you said?

> History is braided like a young woman's hair. She's either
> Evading you or you evade her.
>
> A bit of pink paper is braided in
> By her mother. It says,

"Love surrounds you if you don't make a whore of my daughter."

2669345

Made in the USA